Stefanie has the ability to step outside her pain and describe for those who haven't experienced it the devastation wrought by miscarriage. Her story tells of the loss of a much-wanted pregnancy, but it also tells of the author's spiritual journey. Most poignant are her conversations with her three-year-old daughter, as together they explore what has happened to their family. The reader finds practical strategies mixed in with the struggle as Stefanie tells of her search for emotional stability. The raw reality of her experience is one the reader won't forget.

—Bobbi Junior
Author of *The Reluctant Caregiver*
Mom to angel baby Wendy Lorraine Junior

Stefanie's story gives a courageous voice to the silent cry of mothers (and fathers) whose hearts ache and lament over the loss of their unborn children. It brings to light a topic that is painfully concealed and difficult to discuss in our world. Her words come from a place of vulnerable honesty and are of comfort to those who walk a similar journey.

—Michelle Jones
Mom to three angel babies: Arianna, Asher, and Elijah

Chasing Light is an invaluable and inspiring book that will bring insight, healing, and hope to those who have gone through a miscarriage or who know a loved one who has. Powerful, honest, and captivating, this book is a must-read!

—Sharleen W.
Pastor, Thrive Church
Mom to an angel baby

This story was beautifully honest and raw with emotions coming straight from the heart. Pregnancy loss and depression are not topics often discussed, and I commend Stefanie's courage in doing so. As a mother who has experienced miscarriage, I cried, understanding the sadness and reluctance to seek support. This book gives readers insight into a world that many women experience and few talk about. I hope in reading this more people will feel like they are not alone and that support is available.

—Dorothy T.
Registered Nurse
Mom of an angel baby

Chasing Light

Finding Hope

Through the Loss

of Miscarriage

Stefanie Tong

CHASING LIGHT
Copyright © 2016 by Stefanie Tong

Scripture quotations marked (NIV) are taken from the HOLY BIBLE, NEW INTERNATIONAL VERSION®. NIV®. Copy- right© 1973, 1978, 1984 by International Bible Society. Used by permission of Zondervan. All rights reserved. Scripture quotations marked (NLT) are taken from the Holy Bible, New Living Translation, copyright © 1996, 2004, 2007 by Tyndale House Foundation. Used by permission of Tyndale House Publishers, Inc., Carol Stream, Illinois 60188. All rights reserved.

ISBN: 978-1-4866-1204-8

Word Alive Press
131 Cordite Road, Winnipeg, MB R3W 1S1
www.wordalivepress.ca

Library and Archives Canada Cataloguing in Publication

Tong, Stefanie, 1984-, author
    Chasing light : finding hope through the loss of miscarriage / Stefanie Tong.

Issued in print and electronic formats.
ISBN 978-1-4866-1204-8 (paperback).--ISBN 978-1-4866-1205-5 (pdf).--ISBN 978-1-4866-1206-2 (html).--ISBN 978-1-4866-1207-9 (epub)

    1. Tong, Stefanie, 1984-. 2. Miscarriage--Religious aspects--Christianity. 3. Bereavement--Religious aspects--Christianity. 4. Grief--Religious aspects--Christianity. 5. Mother and child--Religious aspects--Christianity. 6. Christian life. I. Title.

BV4907.T66 2016   248.8'66   C2016-900557-7
                                            C2016-900558-5

Contents

Foreword

Miscarriage—it occurs far more frequently than most people realize. It is probably far less understood than people know, too.

My husband and I, along with a wonderful board of directors, run a bereaved parents support group in Western British Columbia, Canada. Since our own losses in the mid 1990s, we have worked with numerous families for whom miscarriage and pregnancy loss are a harsh reality. The book you are about to read is written by one of those parents. It is the true story of one couple's experience in the world of parenthood. Its candor and honesty show incredible strength and the desire to help others heal by sharing a mutual experience.

If you are reading this book because you have experienced a loss, my heartfelt sympathies go out to you. Know that the loss was *not your fault*! There was most likely nothing you could have done to prevent this from happening. Despite what people may say, a miscarriage is something that happened *to* you, not something you caused.

Healing is something that will take time, so be kind to yourself. There is no timeline. People may cruelly tell you that you have to "get over it" and "get back to normal." What they don't understand is that this is not a cold that you get over. You have lost a part of yourself—someone very important, special, and precious to you. Your baby will forever be a part of you and your family. You will forever be a parent, whether the world sees you that way or not.

You may or may not ever return to what your normal used to be. You will, however, in time achieve a new normal, and this new you will be even more special than the person you were, for a heart broken by grief has a new understanding of how cruel life can be and can become more compassionate to those it encounters.

Your child existed, and it is my belief that one day you will be reunited. For now, know that you were the best parent to your baby in his or her short life as you could possibly be. They knew they were loved, and one day they will be able to thank you in person for being their parent.

Above all, believe that you are not alone in this experience. If you are willing to be vulnerable with those you encounter, not only will your heart find healing, but you will have a huge part to play in bringing miscarriage and pregnancy loss into the light and making it acceptable to acknowledge so that others who have suffered in silence may find healing from their pain.

If you are reading this because someone you know has experienced a loss and you have a desire to support them, you will learn plenty about the feelings associated with this type of grief. It is unique. It takes time to work through and requires love and support by friends and family. Losing a baby, especially if getting pregnant was difficult, is one of life's most devastating experiences.

Not only has the physical pregnancy been lost but also all the hopes and dreams already formed for that child.

Your willingness to offer support will be one of the biggest gifts you can give a friend or family member. Allow them to remember their child. Assure them it is all right to talk about their baby if they want to; it's okay to cry, be angry, or just sit quietly and remember. If a name was chosen for their child, remember to use that name when talking about their baby. You may wish to offer practical help by making or answering phone calls, contacting co-workers with the news, taking older children for a while to give the parents a chance to rest, or providing a meal. Remind the parents that loss takes time to recover from. One day they will smile again, but for now it is enough to just "be."

A caring friend who makes it clear that he or she is willing to listen and be a safe person to bounce thoughts off of is one of life's greatest gifts, so thank you in advance for your willingness to be that person.

This heartfelt and tender book will be helpful to those experiencing loss as well as to their loved ones. By reading this book, you are showing your support for the many families who have experienced loss. From all of us—thank you.

—Nancy Slinn

Empty Cradle Support Group Coordinator

Mom of three angels: Chris, Vic, and Angel

chapter one

A Dimly Lit Room

ANTICIPATION FILLED ME AS I WOKE THAT MONDAY MORNING. We had been waiting patiently for this day to arrive, the day we'd get to see our newly forming baby. I was nine weeks and five days pregnant and was looking forward to the ultrasound.

As instructed, I emptied my bladder when I woke and began to drink the required four cups of water. I wasn't willing to risk having to delay the opportunity to see our little bean. My husband, Brian, and I had a short discussion about whether we should take two cars or one to the appointment. Brian would head to work afterwards, and so would I. Since we would be travelling in opposite directions, we decided to drive separately.

I couldn't wait to come home with a picture to show Maliya and to tell her that she was going to be a big sister. We had decided to keep the news from her for fear of the chatty two-year-old telling everyone "Mommy has a baby in her tummy," but we had been dropping hints for a few weeks. Even though she was only two, Maliya was very intuitive and spiritually sensitive to those around her. She constantly sought information, asking, "How come?" in every conversation. Without speaking at all, Maliya recognized when an adult needed comfort, climbed into the person's lap, and offered encouragement with her gentle words "It's okay." Keeping information from her was no easy task, especially an announcement we were so excited to share.

My doctor had given me the ultrasound requisition five weeks earlier, and I had purposely booked it for around the ninth week of my pregnancy, knowing that we'd be able to see a baby instead of a forming sac. On my drive there I noticed that we were in the final days of summer and began thinking about how our family would change that coming spring. I prayed and I listened to music, but something inside me caused me to be nervous. *Nervous excitement,* I thought. We were going to have another little one to care for.

My mental list began. A crib mattress and a bassinet needed to be purchased, the spare room had to be cleaned, the crib had to be assembled, and we needed to save for my maternity leave. Yes, nerves were warranted. Unknown to me, the Holy Spirit was already interceding on my behalf for this appointment.

As a person who is sensitive to the spirit world, I do not doubt that this trait has been passed on to my daughter. I came to know Jesus ten years ago and since then have had countless spiritual encounters. One can't believe in heaven without acknowledging the existence of hell. I've seen, smelled, touched, and heard things from hell that should only exist in horror movies. The presence of God has also touched me in ways that have moved me to tears. When the Holy Spirit met me on my drive that morning, I knew it was a sign I couldn't ignore.

Arriving at the radiology department, I submitted my requisition form. When my name was called I followed the technician, who told Brian that she'd be back for him in fifteen minutes. I headed into the dimly lit examination room and lay where I was instructed on top of the cold tissue paper, which crunched as I repositioned myself.

Cold jelly was squirted on my belly, and the probe was maneuvered around my abdomen. The technician's face was emotionless. *They're well trained,* I thought.

After a few minutes of pushing around on my belly, she asked how the pregnancy had been going. I said it was normal and that I was feeling nauseated and tired. She then asked if I'd had any spotting. *Well, that's slightly alarming,* I thought. I answered, "Only for a few hours one day, and it was very faint, not enough to show up on a liner." The technician then said that she'd like to do an internal ultrasound since it was still early in the pregnancy; I was to empty my bladder and return for part two.

Having been pregnant before, I knew that at nine weeks a baby should be visible. The level of my concern began to rise. Internal ultrasound? Why? What was wrong?

The second ultrasound began, bringing physical discomfort. Feeling this probe inside of me, turning and twisting while the technician was doing the examination, was not pleasant. From within, I could feel each angle being inspected, every poke, every glide, forward and backward.

The technician was still not showing any emotion. She then told me I could get dressed and that she'd be right back. Where was she going? She hadn't even shown me the monitor yet. I wanted to see my baby!

Obviously, at this point, my concerns were growing and I knew something was wrong. I sent a text message to Brian, who was still in the waiting room, and told him what had happened so far. Unable to fully grasp the situation, all I could tell him was that this appointment wasn't going right and that I didn't understand the technician's actions.

I wished Brian was with me. Thirty feet down a narrow hall separated us. Helpless, I stood alone in the eerie dim room, the hum of the imaging machine being overpowered by my lurking fear.

The technician came back and closed the door behind her. She said, "We're calling your doctor right now. I can't discuss what I saw, but your doctor will know in ten minutes, and I suggest you visit your doctor this afternoon."

A work supervisor used to tell me that I should never play poker, for I lack the ability to hide how I feel. I knew the technician could read my facial expression, which begged, "Just tell me what's going on; I can handle it!" She said again, "I'm really sorry I can't tell you what I saw, but you can call your doctor in twenty minutes. She'll know by then."

Know what? What's going on? "Is it still in there?" I asked.

She replied, "Something is in there; I can't say any more, but you can call your doctor shortly."

I forced myself to thank her as she left the examination room, though inside I was raging. It felt inhumane to leave the conversation in such a manner, withholding vital information from me, information about me and my baby. My heart was pounding, and the nervousness from the drive to the appointment had become anxiety. I saw Brian in the waiting room and couldn't even talk to him. I just signaled to him that we had to leave. I walked out of the office quickly, not even checking to see if he was behind me. I knew something was wrong, very wrong.

We stood in the parking lot, and I told Brian everything that had happened and everything that was said. "At nine weeks the technician shouldn't have had to do an internal ultrasound; it doesn't make sense. What was she looking for?" I wondered.

Then it clicked. "I don't think she could find a heartbeat." Emotions rose from my heart to my throat, and I severed them before they could reach my eyes, where they would have surely poured out.

We waited twenty minutes and then called my doctor's office. The receptionist informed me that Dr. J wasn't in, but if my ultrasound results were urgent, the radiologist would contact my doctor directly and I would receive a call from Dr. J. I tried to convince myself that there was nothing urgent.

Feeling physically ill, I decided not to work that day and headed home. The morning had only begun, but I wished for the day to be over. Thankfully, I could lie in bed and rest while my mother-in-law spent the day with Maliya.

There was no phone call that day. That night, tears rolled down my face as I tried to sleep. The optimist in me was being overpowered by what I had witnessed. Could I be having a miscarriage? Tension filled my body as that thought cycled through my mind. I hadn't bled or had any cramps, only some discomfort when I went to bed the day I had spotted.

The following morning, Brian asked me to call the doctor's office again. This time the receptionist informed me that Dr. J was out of the office until the following day and that my message was still there from the previous day. She wasn't able to confirm if the ultrasound results had been received. We faced another day of waiting.

I knew God was inviting us to draw closer to Him in prayer. My prayers grew shorter as the day went on. By the end of the day, I had no words for God at all. My human emotions had taken over. I was annoyed. I was sad. I was anxious. Waiting was unbearable, though waiting still gave me hope.

chapter two

The Call

I'M NOT EVEN SURE IF I SLEPT THAT NIGHT. FEELING LIKE A zombie, I got up with Maliya the next morning and kept my phone close to me. Knowing that Dr. J would be back in the office that day, I didn't want to chance missing any calls.

We got ready for the day and had our breakfast, and my in-laws took Maliya out for the morning. My plan was to tidy a few things and head to work. Then my phone buzzed with a voice message notification. *Odd*, I thought, *my phone never rang.*

I was nervous punching in the numbers to access my voice message. There was only one call that I was expecting, since no one else would call me first thing in the morning.

It was Dr. J. My heart sank upon hearing that she wanted me to call her back immediately. By the end of the voice message my heart was racing, and I promptly called her office. It rang once, and Dr. J picked up with a "Hello?" This told me she was expecting my call too, which made my heart sink to my stomach.

She asked how I was doing, and I wasn't sure how to answer. I replied that I was okay. She apologized for not getting back to me sooner, as she saw I had been calling. I knew it was no fault of hers for being out of the office and began to tell her what happened at the ultrasound, mostly that the technician launched me into panic mode.

Dr. J said she was going to ask the receptionist to call me in for an afternoon appointment but didn't want me to have to wait all day. I interrupted and said, "We're already expecting the worst."

She replied, "I didn't want to tell you this over the phone, but you're right. Unfortunately, the ultrasound didn't show a heartbeat; the pregnancy is not viable. I'm so sorry."

I stood there in the middle of my bedroom, frozen. Even though we had already been expecting this, hearing it confirmed was heart-wrenching.

Breaking the silence, Dr. J began to offer some medical explanations for miscarriages. She also reminded me that I had been very sick at the beginning of my pregnancy with a stomach virus, which likely contributed to the miscarriage. My body was trying to purge a virus while DNA was being knit together in my womb, and my body may have just purged everything. I was thankful that Dr. J, who was so gentle in delivering the news, took the time to counsel me over the phone and began advising me of the next steps.

The diagnosis was a missed miscarriage; this meant that my baby was still inside of me. With an appointment already scheduled for the following day, Dr. J said she'd let me digest our conversation and would meet with me then, and if I needed anything to please call her. The next day's appointment had originally been planned for discussing the next steps in my pregnancy, to order blood tests and set up more prenatal appointments. Instead, my visit would be to discuss which method I'd like to choose to complete my miscarriage, to empty my uterus.

I thanked Dr. J again for taking the time to call. I definitely felt cared for and not rushed through any of my questions.

With my heart feeling like it was going to pound right out of my chest, I sent Brian a text message to tell him that I had just gotten off the phone with the doctor. He let me know he'd step out of the office to call me. This conversation was a blur. My emotions were running high, and I don't recall much of what was said. One thing I do remember was Brian repeatedly asking me if I wanted him to come home to be with me. I declined his offer because I wasn't sure what I wanted in that moment, to be alone to process the news or to be held and comforted. Brian reassured me that we would get through this, that we had gone through so much already, and that we'd face this together as well. With that, he hung up, and I had enough strength in me for one more phone call, to my mom.

Since our parents were over on weekdays as our childcare providers, we had told them as soon as we found out we were pregnant. Trying to collect myself, I took a big, long breath before the phone call.

I could tell that my mom was surprised to hear from me, as I'd usually already be at work. At a loss for words, I blurted out, "I had a miscarriage."

My mom was silent for a moment and then replied, "Oh, Stef."

After filling her in on a few details from my conversation with the doctor and the events of the ultrasound, I quickly switched modes to give her instructions. She would be coming over that night to help me with Maliya. Brian would be at school, and with my back still not recovered from the most recent rear-end car accident (there have been three rear-enders in total), my mom and stepdad had been helping me on the evenings when I was on my own.

The instructions I had for my mom that evening were to not discuss or mention anything I had just told her about and in fact to please not even hug me because I'd probably break down and not be able to function afterwards, and to please tell my stepdad for me because I wouldn't be able to repeat this story another time.

chapter three

Alone

I ENDED THE CALL WITH MY MOM AND SAT AT THE EDGE OF MY bed in disbelief. So far I had held it together for the doctor's call, sharing the news with Brian, and telling my mom. "Now what?" I was supposed to be at work, but there was no way I'd be heading out the door in my current state to serve 107 families as the manager of a preschool. There are certain expectations of someone in that role: a smiling face, a welcoming spirit, and a nurturing heart. Parents often seek advice from me, and children look to me for security, creativity, and consistency. I could not be that person that day.

With a pen and paper, I lay on my stomach on my carpeted bedroom floor. The light on that cloudy day peeked in through the curtain opening just enough for me to jot down my thoughts on the page.

Music flowed in from the next room as I stared with intent at the blank paper in front of me. How could I even begin to put into words what I was feeling? The rhythm playing brought me back to the days when music and dance were my escape and to a time when I taught dance and used hip-hop movements to counsel myself through any emotional situation. Usually I would've danced out any emotions, but with the recent car accident, any physical activity outside of walking and my rehabilitation exercises was prohibited by my physiotherapist.

I have an incredibly strong will in the way that I can manipulate my feelings and shut them off. (It's my downfall and a self-defence tool at the same time.) This was the first time I couldn't do that. My heart was utterly broken, and no amount of strength from my mind could turn off what I was feeling.

We had prayed for eight months before trying to conceive. Eight months of praying that our will would align with God's to bring a life into the world. When we conceived within the first month of trying, we felt that God was answering our prayers about timing and had used the eight months of prayer to prepare us for being parents of a newborn again. How could everything that felt so right now be so wrong?

Alone in my room, I wondered if I should use the time to write about how shocked I was that God allowed this to happen. Three car accidents, ten years of chronic back pain, and now a miscarriage. "Lord, how much more do You think I can take? I've had my share of pain, and still there's more?" I could relate to the story of Job in the Bible, yet, lying there on the floor, I couldn't talk to God. I was too distraught to acknowledge that He was even there. In my anger, I chose to ignore Him. I felt forsaken.

The first words I got down on the page were "little you," words for my baby, a poem, simply because full sentences seemed impossible. By the second stanza, I was crying hysterically. Tears rushed down my cheeks like a waterfall. I couldn't wipe them away fast enough to see in front of me. Within seconds, I was shaking and had a headache. A pool of my tears collected near the bottom of the page. It was silly of me to think I'd have any other reaction. After holding it together for two long days waiting for the doctor's call and for three phone conversations that repeatedly used the word "miscarriage," I was finally alone, and it was safe to release what I had held captive. Completing my downpour of tears, I resumed writing.

Somehow, after creating the poem, writing to my little one, and blaming God, I picked myself up off the ground and went to work. Ludicrous, I know, but I didn't know what else to do.

chapter four

The Prescription

THE NEXT DAY DR. J TOLD ME THE ULTRASOUND SHOWED THAT our baby had stopped growing at six weeks of gestation. Since our little one's body still had not passed, I opted for medication that I would administer at home to complete the miscarriage. Possible side effects included vomiting, diarrhea, and fever, on top of what the drug was designed to do, send my body into labour. Dr. J warned that it would be painful and that she usually prescribed a painkiller for this process. Then she said, "Knowing you, you wouldn't wake up until next Tuesday if I prescribed anything for you."

This observation was absolutely true. I regularly get side effects from medication. Unlike during the induced labour with Maliya (which, of course, I had a reaction to), I could at least take pain medication this time. A combination of over-the-counter painkillers was what I decided on.

The prescription for misoprostol was ready the following day, and the pharmacy was unavoidable, as I'd be passing by on my regular route home. Picking up the prescription brought on enough anxiety to suffocate me. My biggest fear was running into one of my preschool families. Living in the same community as I work in can be a challenge at times. I enjoy connecting with all the families I've met over the years and getting to see those three-year-olds become teenagers, but running into people I know is unavoidable. To date, I've worked with over one thousand families, so the probability of being recognized is high. Thankfully, I didn't run into anyone I knew that day. No one asked me "How are you?" or "What's new?"

I already loathed those questions. How was I supposed to answer? "Fine"? Well, I definitely wasn't fine. "Not bad"? I guess that was more honest—I wasn't bad; I was horrible and constantly on the verge of tears. Asking in return how he or she was, such a simple question and a regular part of our North American culture, was way beyond my capacity. How could I begin to listen to someone else share about his or her life when mine was falling apart? Simply put, I couldn't.

When the pharmacist called me over, she asked if I had taken this medication before. "No," I replied, with my eyes shifting to the ground.

Misoprostol is commonly used for stomach ulcers. The young pharmacist began to read the label. "So what you're going to do is take four of these pills and *insert*—?" Her eyes grew wide and shock filled her voice as she said, "insert." I assume that she had never counselled on misoprostol being used to complete a miscarriage. She quietly read the rest of the label to herself and then began to advise me again. "So, what you're going to do is wash your hands really well …" Thankfully, Dr. J had prepared me for the process, so I knew what to expect. I felt like I needed to counsel the pharmacist after she read that label!

That night, I contemplated how much dinner I should be having if this drug was going to have me expel my stomach contents in a few hours. Doctors are good at preparing you for the worst, aren't they? Mine also warned that if I began bleeding too much, I would need to head to the hospital, so that was another thought looming in my mind.

At 8:00 p.m. I told Brian that he should prepare to be in solo parenting mode. I picked up the prescription bottle and stared at the little white hexagonal pills, knowing what was ahead of me that evening. Two doses were prescribed in case the first dose wasn't successful.

I had a long shower and felt tears rolling off my face. Crying would not bring our baby back. This immense pain was unbearable. Down the drain I washed my tears along with my dreams and plans for our second child. I'd never get to hold or kiss my baby or watch Maliya be an older sister to our second child.

I used my mind to push myself forward to administer the medication. I knew if I followed my heart, I'd be in a ball on the bathroom floor. My heart felt like someone had punched it, ripped it out, stomped on it, and then made it a target for firearms practice. I looked at the little white pills and made one request to God. "No side effects, Lord; just let these pills do what they have to." My cry was both a plea and a threat.

After administering the medication, I did as instructed and lay down so that gravity wouldn't be working against my body. Maliya was playing in the living room, and I surrounded myself with pillows and watched her from the couch. Nothing seemed to be happening to my body particularly—no cramps—so after thirty minutes I decided to get up. That's when it started, the immense and immediate pain. What I was feeling wasn't cramps; I was having contractions. I told Brian that I was heading upstairs and that the end of my day had arrived. The end of carrying our baby had arrived.

Alone, I retreated to our bedroom and crawled into our bed, where this little being had been created. The beginning and ending of a life was so much closer together than we ever imagined. I dosed myself with a combination of ibuprofen and acetaminophen and tried to sleep it off. That's right, I tried to sleep off self-induced labour to complete a miscarriage. Needless to say, I was up and down all night.

I remember the following morning like it was yesterday. I felt something leave my body, and I rushed to the bathroom. Miscarriage complete. There in my hands was my baby, our baby, complete in his or her forming sac. "Baby, is that you?" I whispered. Thankfully nothing really resembled a human; otherwise, I would have entered a new level of devastation in the midst of the existing emotional torment. Still, I cradled in my hands what was supposed to be thriving inside of me. Part of me didn't want to let go, as this was my only opportunity to hold our second child. My mind was telling me to move on, my heart was holding on, and then my mind kicked in again and told me to stop staring at a blob that had just come out of my body. With that, I gave my final goodbye to the little love whom I will only get to meet when I enter heaven.

chapter five

Questions

FOR SEVERAL WEEKS I LIVED IN UTTER CONFUSION, NOT knowing what to do, whether I was supposed to carry on or let myself mourn. Days seemed like weeks, and weeks seemed like months. The first two weeks were absolutely clouded, and, with no courage to tell anyone about our miscarriage, we lacked the support we needed. It's still unclear to me why miscarriage is such a taboo topic when clearly anyone going through the loss of a child needs a large network of support.

Tears flowed daily, sometimes at rather inconvenient moments, like at work or while purchasing groceries. Crawling into a hole and hiding for a few weeks seemed like a great coping strategy but not practical with a two-year-old to care for. Had Maliya not needed me and made me laugh, I might very well still be in that hole I craved.

I thought that completing the miscarriage would give me a sense of peace, but I had another ultrasound looming over my head. There was a lot of fear going into that appointment. The ultrasound requisition tore my heart apart emotionally. Dr. J told me, "Please don't be alarmed at the medical term for a missed miscarriage, which is 'missed abortion.'" The requisition read,

"Follow up missed spontaneous abortion. Patient did a course of misoprostol. Ensure full passage of POCs."

I pinned the requisition to my bulletin board and stared at it until my appointment day, still in disbelief of my situation. Since I didn't know what "POC" stood for, I quickly entered the letters in an online search engine. My heart sank when I read that POC stands for "products of conception." In medical terms, our baby was nothing more than a product of conception, and the life we prayed for ended in what was deemed an abortion. These words were the harsh heart-wrenching truth.

What if my body hadn't done what it was supposed to after using the medication? What if not everything had cleared? What if I had to get a D and C (dilatation and curettage)? My thoughts spiralled. Dr. J said if I needed a D and C, our city would not consider it an emergency procedure, and I'd be put on a wait-list. While I waited, I'd have to fast each night, just in case I got a phone call confirming the procedure the following morning. If there was no phone call, there would be no procedure. In my mind, she had just described hell to me.

Sadness and anxiety followed me to the ultrasound appointment. I entered a familiar room with another silent technician. After pushing around with the ultrasound probe and capturing a few images, the technician asked, "Are you still bleeding?"

"No."

"Then I'd like to do an internal ultrasound. Everything looks clear, but I just want to double-check."

It was another unpleasant experience, but thankfully the ultrasound showed that my uterus was clear, which I took as a sign that God was indeed taking care of me. My fears of a possible D and C could be laid to rest.

Knowing that everything was healthy inside still did not give me peace. My cramping continued on and off. Every cramp was a reminder that my baby was gone. I endured each one in silence and didn't even tell Brian. Reality was striking me at random moments and bringing me into the depths of my loss. I could hardly breathe at times, and other times I could've punched people in the face.

"So are you guys gonna have another one?" "Do you think you'll have another baby?" "When is your next one coming?" Since when was this anyone else's business? In the weeks following the miscarriage, every time I was faced with a question like this, I held back tears.

I forced myself to politely reply, "We'll have another one when the timing is right," when really I wanted to clench my fist and forcefully direct it toward their faces.

Emotional triggers seemed to be everywhere. It felt impossible to guard my heart. I either hid behind a shield of anxiety and terror, waiting for questions about having another child, or let my guard down, only to be blindsided. Finding the middle ground seemed unattainable.

When I was told "It's about time for you to have another one," I felt like I was being held at gunpoint. There were no warning signs, and suddenly I was backed into a corner with my arms up, heart racing, breath expelled, and full of panic. Some days I was tempted to look at the questioner and say, "Just pull it. Just pull the trigger, because I'd rather have no emotions at all than feel this excruciating heartache."

This practice of asking about when others are having children is somehow a societal norm. Is it possible to break this convention? Even before the miscarriage, I never asked others unless they brought it up first. I don't think it's any of my business when people decide to have their children or not to have any children at all. Before asking a woman about when she plans to have a baby, I consider that she may have been trying to conceive for years and faced disappointment and grief month after month. Marked calendars, fertility tests, hormone therapies, and artificial insemination are not guarantees of carrying a life for nine months before bringing a baby into the world. I know there are mothers who have recently lost their babies and are suffering in silence, who are absolutely sick in their spirits because they have experienced multiple losses. Why would I ever want to throw this intrusive question around in a conversation following "How are you?"

These trials are invisible and wear a person down. The women who have lost their children to miscarriages are mothers who will never get to hold those children. They will never be celebrated by the world around them on Mother's Day for the baby they lost, will never hear the word "Mama" from the lost child's lips, and will live daily in unseen emotional turmoil.

chapter six

Malakai

ABOUT ONE MONTH AFTER MY MISCARRIAGE, I STAYED UP LATE one evening to answer emails from friends who were meeting me in my sadness. I'm so thankful for my girlfriends who took the time to write long emails even though pregnancy was foreign to them. They reminded me of God's goodness and helped me to see His glory in the situation.

In the middle of responding to emails, I found myself on a naming website. I don't even know how I ended up there. When I was pregnant with Maliya, for a long time the only name we considered was "Malakai." If we were to have a boy, Malakai would be his name; if we were to have a girl, we had no clue what her name would be. I had no plans for the name of the baby we lost. We had been calling him or her our "angel" because we didn't know whether the baby was a boy or a girl.

As I scrolled through many names, I sat in my loss and told myself to move on; there was no longer a baby to name. Just then, "Malakai" popped into my mind, so I typed in the name to find its meaning. The words "my angel" popped up on my screen, and I completely broke down. I cried in silence, as Maliya and Brian were already asleep. Tears flooded my eyes, cascaded down my cheeks, and ended up being absorbed by the sleeves of my pajamas. My angel, Malakai.

At that moment, God spoke clearly to me. He said that even before we had Maliya, He knew this miscarriage would happen, and the name we had selected was chosen in heaven long before any of this was revealed to us. God told me that we had a son. In that moment God let me know I was not forsaken and He had never left me; He is the same yesterday, today, and forever (Hebrews 13:8).

It was well after midnight, but I had to tell Brian. I quietly crawled into bed, tapped Brian on the shoulder, and apologized for waking him, but what I had to say couldn't wait. Trying to make sense of what just happened, I told him about how God led me to go to the naming website and to type in the name "Malakai." "God is telling us we have a son."

"Well, I guess we can't use that name anymore," Brian whispered through his tears.

"We just did."

chapter seven

Depression

M Y DOCTOR KEPT A CLOSE EYE ON ME AFTER THE MISCARRIAGE. Her compassion and quality of care made me feel valued and validated. She wanted to ensure that I wouldn't, in her words, "spiral downwards." As a mother of two herself, she could tell that my heart was shattered.

One month after the miscarriage, I had a checkup for my back, in regards to the car accident. Dr. J spent most of the appointment asking about my mood. She knew I had already been feeling low because of the slow recovery of my back, and five months before she had written a prescription for clinical counselling. She mentioned antidepressants and said I could think about it. At the end of the appointment, she handed over three weeks' worth of medication for me to try.

Losses associated with the third car accident had already led me to being depressed. The miscarriage warranted the help of medication to regulate me, but her recommendation of antidepressants upset me. My heart sank upon learning that medical intervention was needed, and my mind spiralled.

Immediately my thoughts led me to the spirit realm, where I had been attacked by evil many times before. I believe nightmares, immoral thoughts, and even sudden physical ailments are attacks on my spirit by creatures of a different realm. I believe in the operation of three realms. We live on earth, the natural realm, where concepts like time and age exist. In this realm, we coexist with angels and demons, which enter and exit earth many times without us knowing. In the past when I have shared my eerie experiences with friends, many of them have said, "Sometimes I get the feeling that something is following me." Without trying to alarm them I would reply, "Because something probably is." Unfortunately, I've had too many encounters with the faces of evil to discount its existence.

The second realm is the spirit realm, where the fight between good and evil is constant. This realm, unseen by the naked eye, is where angels and demons war. To see spirit beings with your naked eye is a blessing or a curse, depending on the person who is experiencing it. I don't often see into this realm with my naked eye but do so with my mind's eye, particularly through visions and dreams. We all have a destiny. Demons try to hinder us from reaching our destiny, while angels try to protect us on our journey.

Heaven is the final realm, where I believe we were fearfully and wonderfully made (Psalm 139) and where we will return when this temporary life is over.

When Dr. J said that it would be four to six weeks before I'd experience benefits from the antidepressants, I couldn't help but question if I was really clinically depressed. Perhaps I had become a pawn in a game between demons; one evil tormented my body while another manipulated my mind. If so, I wondered if medication would help at all. Perhaps all I needed to do was pray. The medication could make me completely drowsy or extremely wired, and it would likely make me nauseous as well. My hormones were just starting to return to normal, and the thought of being nauseous all over again did not appeal to me, especially since it didn't involve the promise of holding a baby at the end.

Brian thought I should have been on antidepressants weeks earlier. He just wanted his wife back, no matter what it took. After finding the courage to tell our Bible study group about the miscarriage, I shared openly about my depression and received a lot of support and opinions. This helped me compare the advantages and disadvantages of antidepressants, and I also discussed their pros and cons with each one of my healthcare professionals. I finally decided not to take them for the time being.

One of the largest contributing factors to my decision was knowing that we wanted to conceive again. I didn't want to start any medication only to have to wean off it to get pregnant. Dr. J explained that I could be on antidepressants while pregnant, but the risks were higher for respiratory problems for the baby after birth, which could mean a longer hospital stay. After losing Malakai, those risks were not worth it to me. No risk during pregnancy would be worth it. Since I was not a danger to myself or to others, Dr. J continued to leave this decision up to me. (Please note, I am not suggesting that antidepressants aren't necessary in some situations. I was under the care of my family doctor, a chronic pain specialist, a physiotherapist, and a clinical counsellor, who were assessing my situation weekly.)

As I battled with depression, Brian and I grieved together and secluded ourselves for months because being in a social setting was too difficult. It was painful to be asked if we were planning to expand our family, and infants were constant reminders of our loss. There were many weeks when we chose not to attend church. I couldn't pretend to worship the Lord when I was so angry with Him, though He constantly reminded us—through emails and cards from the few people we had the courage to share our story with—that we were cared for. By His grace, I found the strength to attend Bible study regularly. The smaller group size helped, but I felt like the rebel in the group, constantly challenging the gospel and what I previously believed. I didn't doubt that God existed, but having faith was a difficult concept when I felt like everything I had prayed for had been taken away.

We declined social invitations, and I felt horrible for not attending two of my good friends' baby showers, but I knew I wouldn't survive. There was absolutely no way I could sustain myself for three hours while playing baby games, knowing that a life should have been growing inside of me. Even though my friends knew the reason I couldn't attend, I still felt selfish. I wish I could've stepped outside of myself to celebrate with my friends, but I couldn't. This decision left me feeling guilty.

No one at work knew what I was going through. I couldn't bring myself to tell them. Every morning I prayed that I would make it through the day serving families with young children. Some days I stared at my work; minutes would pass by, and I'd be completely lost, forgetting what task I had started. The trauma from the miscarriage was unexpected. I prayed for God's mercy and that He would help me hold it together as parents carried their infants into our classrooms to pick up their older children.

Others would swoon over these little ones, and I wished I could giggle over them as I had just weeks before. It was by His strength and not my own that I made it to work at all.

chapter eight

I Want to Go There

ONE OF THE MOST DIFFICULT THINGS IN THE MIDST OF MY grief was trying to stay composed for Maliya in order to provide the consistent routine that she was used to. Pretending that everything was normal at home was tearing me apart. She saw me cry, and I'd just tell her that I was sad. How could I tell a two-year-old that there had been a baby in my womb, but now there wasn't?

Brian and I discussed whether we should tell her about the baby, and we decided that we would, if an opportunity should present itself. It broke me to keep such a big part of my life from my daughter.

Maliya is a little love who requires *a lot* of nighttime parenting— actually, a lot of nighttime mommying. When I'm in the house, it's guaranteed that I'm the one putting her to bed. She also requires an adult to stay with her until she falls asleep. As if that's not enough, she often needs some form of physical touch, holding my hand, playing footsies, or wrapping herself around my arm.

After our bedtime prayers one night, I told her I'd be reading a book and to please go to sleep. This was the moment God opened up for me to tell her that she was a big sister to a baby in heaven.

"What you gonna read?"

"A story about heaven. Do you believe heaven is real?"

"Yeah."

"That's where Jesus lives." I took a deep breath and continued, "I have something to tell you." Now I had a two-year-old staring at me with wide eyes. "Mama had a baby in my tummy, but now the baby is in heaven with Jesus."

"What's his name?"

Did Maliya receive a revelation that the baby was a boy? Was God using her as affirmation? I couldn't believe how naturally she asked what "his" name was, as if she knew. "Malakai."

"I want to see him."

"I know; me too. One day we'll all be together."

"Is he sick?"

"Yeah, he was a little sick; he wasn't growing, so Jesus will help him grow in heaven until we get there."

"Did he throw up?"

"No, he didn't throw up," I replied through my laughter.

"Where's heaven?"

"Way up in the sky."

"I want to go there."

"One day we will. It's far away."

"I have to drive there. Did the baby not try come out?"

"The baby came out and went right to heaven, but he wasn't big enough for us to see. He died in Mama's tummy."

"I want to see it died."

"No, we won't get to see the baby on earth, but he's living with Jesus in heaven."

"I want to see the baby."

"One day. One day we'll all get to see the baby. Thank you for letting me tell you, Maliya." And with that, she was content and rolled over to go to sleep.

chapter nine

Behind Closed Doors

THREE MONTHS PASSED BEFORE I COULD UTTER THE WORD "miscarriage." Even behind closed doors at my counselling sessions, I could barely bring myself to talk about it. I had been in counselling before for the trauma associated with my first two car accidents, and when Dr. J handed me a list of resources for counselling this time, I knew I needed a Christian to take this journey with me. With many questions about God, His plans for me, and my lack of trust in Him, I needed someone to help me unpack my faith. Since angels and demons had also been very present in my faith journey, I didn't want to be put in a psychiatric ward for mentioning the supernatural things I had experienced.

Finding a Christian counsellor in my city wasn't easy. Only one name came up in my online searches, but it would mean a thirty-minute drive into Vancouver, which was difficult with my constant back flare-ups. I called around and found another in Burnaby, which was a forty-five-minute drive away. Finally, a counselling service returned my call and told me about a counselling practice in my city, located inside a church that many of my friends attended.

That night I went through all the online biographies of the counsellors available at the centre. Juliana has a master of arts degree in marriage and family therapy, specializes in loss, anger, and grief, and has additional training in trauma. I decided to see if she was accepting new clients and was in her office within one week. It has been an emotional and spiritual journey ever since.

Juliana constantly challenged me to find a place where I could experience an emotion with both my heart and my mind instead of my default, which was using my mind to override my heart and pull myself out of my feelings. My Christian ideologies constantly pulled me away from feeling my emotions. I wouldn't allow myself to experience sadness, anger, or depression, because my mind and spirit knew that, through Jesus, I had already claimed victory over my trials. It made me feel less of a Christian to sit in my lows when God is so much bigger than my worldly dilemmas. However, my heart didn't trust God, while my head consistently battled what I was feeling.

In Juliana's words to my doctor, "We have been doing trauma work, internal emotional work, tracing emotional responses and seeking to gently monitor the psychosomatic connections in order to identify where the emotional blockages or disconnects might be, and how they might be contributing to the physical flare-ups." Just when I felt I was making progress, the word "miscarriage" entered our sessions, and I was thrown right back into the centre of my trauma.

Each week I left counselling with homework. It was no easy task, trying to trace my emotions and give them the space they needed. My first homework assignment was to schedule a time to cry.

I failed that assignment. It seemed ludicrous to visit the past, connect with some memory that would evoke tears, enter that space, and let the tears fall to complete that cycle of thoughts and emotions. Anxiety is rising in my body now just thinking about that task.

At the end of my second session, Juliana asked if I was familiar with Psalm 88. I was unable to recall the theme of the psalm, and my homework was to read it and write my own psalm of lament. Since then, I have showed up each week with a stack of papers. While it has been daunting to see my file grow thicker, I know that I've contributed to it weekly. Though those pieces are highly emotional and deep in despair, I enjoyed getting lost in the creative process.

The chronic pain clinic I was attending for my back injury offered pain education courses, and I chose to take art therapy. That course gave me homework each week too, while daily tasks included doodling or writing in my sketchbook. With this new tool, I was bringing even more paperwork to my counselling sessions. When poems wouldn't come, I was thankful that I had the creative outlet of my sketchbook.

It took me about eight weeks, but I finally started to connect my artwork to my emotions. We found that through writing I was able to keep both my mind and my heart present, where they could function together without overwhelming me.

While a whole team of health professionals was treating me, I was also under the spiritual care of one of the associate pastors at our church. Pastor Kathy, who met with me about every six weeks, had an incredible way of inviting Jesus into any situation I was facing. I felt a lot of oppression and additional weight after the miscarriage, like something was following me around, and Pastor Kathy could see it when I walked into her office. I didn't even have to mention that my spirit felt under attack; Pastor Kathy already knew what I was going through. Demonic forces were trying to shred me apart, to keep me from operating as a whole. My body felt ripped from my mind and spirit, making me feel mentally and emotionally weak for months. I felt like Humpty Dumpty. We prayed for God to piece me back together again.

chapter ten

War Zone

I was in a dark place for many months and was tormented in my sleep. I had kept a dream journal since I was in high school, and in the months after the miscarriage I recorded nightmares in which I encountered snakes, sharks, and bees. As a frequent dreamer, I took a dream interpretation course years ago based on the biblical teaching about dreams and visions. The creatures I had been seeing all represented demonic activity trying to strike fear in me and withhold me from my destiny.

In one vision, I saw myself walking through dark bushes. Thorns surrounded me but never cut my flesh. While I walked in the dark wilderness, I could barely see what was in front of me. The only lights were glowing eyes that surrounded me as I tried to find my way out.

Brian told me about a vision he had. He saw himself on a boat in the middle of the ocean. A storm surrounded him. The waters were rough, gusty winds were blowing, and the sails on the boat were tattered. While his vision occurred on the water's surface, I had a recurring vision of myself underneath the water. The surface and light weren't far above me, but I was shackled to the ocean floor. I had no desire to break free, and I wasn't panicked.

The sad reality was that I had lost hope and my will to fight and felt completely defeated.

In my sleep, voices from hell taunted me and demons trapped me. Shadows lurked, noticing that I was too low to fight back. Darkness surrounded me even when I walked where the sun gleamed. I lacked patience with myself and preferred to remain numb. If I had had the choice, I would have blasted through this season of mourning, suffering, darkness, and hopelessness. In the depths of my being I didn't want to acknowledge all the emotional torment. I much preferred to disconnect and function apart from my experiences.

In my early twenties, as a new follower of Jesus, I had believed that when tragedy occurred in my life, God was punishing me for my former sins. The enemy succeeded in lying to me, convincing me that I somehow deserved the physical and emotional pain I was enduring.

I was furious with Satan. He was warring against me without mercy. Like in my vision of me underwater, I had no time to come up for air. If I had come up for a breath, the enemy would have swung for the total knockout. I blamed Satan for the pain, the depression, and the miscarriage. Then I realized that his scheme all along was for me to focus on the negative and remain low. I gave him way more attention than I should have. The Holy Spirit helped me realize that focusing so much on Satan's schemes only made me highlight the enemy. Coming to that realization helped me find the will to fight again.

In this season of suffering, I longed to have someone to blame. It was easy to blame both Satan and God. One caused all my misery, and the other allowed it to happen. I slowly let go of the need to blame and accepted the truth that we live in a fallen world, which means sickness, lies, heartache, evil, and death. I've learned that we have a loving and gracious God, one who weeps with us and mourns with us, who has plans to prosper us and not harm us (Jeremiah 29:11). Believing otherwise only makes me agree with Satan's lies.

The god of this world is Satan (2 Corinthians 4:4), and he will plant doubt and deception, highlighting the areas in life where we feel lack. The ruler of the world wants me to think that I am to blame for my miscarriage, that depression is here to stay, and that I will never receive physical healing from my car accidents. I struggle with the thought of never being able to carry another pregnancy to term. The fear is immobilizing. While I acknowledge these things, I don't have to accept them, and they do not define me. My identity is in Christ, who speaks truth and tells me that I am loved (Romans 8:38-39), I am seen (Psalm 33:13-14), my cries are heard (Psalm 116:1-6), I am never forsaken (Deuteronomy 31:6), and I have a purpose (Romans 8:28).

We are in the midst of a spiritual war in which Satan schemes daily to torment our souls, and I was too injured to fight. My armour (Ephesians 6:10–17) was severely damaged, and I needed to patch up the holes where I was wounded, but I couldn't do it alone. I also believed the lie that I had to endure the miscarriage by myself, that no one would want to hear about my loss, that I'd only be seeking attention if I reached out. My spirit was completely wounded for two weeks after our miscarriage, and I chose to seclude myself from others. I was not the mother I wanted to be, the wife I desired to be, or the person I needed to be.

We were created for community by a relational God (Genesis 1:26). He does not want us to be alone, and He sent His Son so that we can have a relationship with Him, an open invitation to eternity.

First Peter 4:12–13 reminds us,

Dear friends, do not be surprised at the fiery ordeal that has come on you to test you, as though something strange were happening to you. But rejoice inasmuch as you participate in the sufferings of Christ, so that you may be overjoyed when his glory is revealed.

When life's trials occurred, I found myself questioning why they were happening. How could I be involved in another rear-end car accident? A miscarriage? Depression? Were these things really happening? I was shocked at how life had unfolded, but these verses tell us to not be surprised at trials and suffering as if something bizarre were happening. Suffering *is* going to happen. The promise I cling to lies in another realm, where supernatural hope originates.

Though we live in the natural realm, I don't believe it's natural to have hope and faith. They are supernatural. Hope and faith are difficult concepts to cling to as humans. We hope not for things we already have but for things that are yet to come (Romans 8:24-25). Hope keeps us in tune to heaven's revelations. Pierre Teilhard de Chardin said, "We are spiritual beings having a human experience,"[1] and I agree wholeheartedly. The earth is our temporary home, with borrowed bodies.

The only way I was able to live in hope and faith was by continually seeking it in the spirit because circumstances and emotions kept me tied to this fallen world. This world reminded me of my hurt, my pain, and my loss. I was tired of the constant fight, and I wanted to give up. Some days I felt ready for heaven. I think Brian and I both did, which left us with unbearable guilt because we had our perfect little three-year-old here on earth.

Faith meant that we were trusting in the unseen and believing in an army of angels fighting alongside us. We were weak, tired, and wounded and nearly became casualties of war.

---

1 *Pierre Teilhard de Chardin*, quoted in Michael Schacker, *Global Awakening: New Science and 21st Century Enlightenment* (Rochester, Vermont: Park Street Press, 2013).

chapter eleven

Unwritten Stories

ONE AFTERNOON I SAT IN PASTOR KATHY'S OFFICE AND TOLD her about a conversation I had with Jesus. He had told me to share my story, to tell others about our miscarriage, and that my story was meant to be public. I'm sure I stopped breathing at that point, because the thought of sharing my story paralyzed me. God was telling me—not asking or inviting, but commanding me—to tell people about my miscarriage.

I said, "No thanks, God. You can go ask someone else, because I'm pretty sure You have the wrong person."

Every day this nagging feeling of being called lived within me, convicting me to share my story with the people around me or, worse, with strangers. Nothing about what God was asking felt safe; it was far out of my comfort zone. I ignored God's requests for many months, but His voice only grew stronger.

When I first told Pastor Kathy about my miscarriage, she said that pregnancy loss was overwhelming our church community; I was the fourth person that month to sit in her office and share her story. My heart broke, knowing that so many others were enduring the same circumstance, yet I didn't know their names and had no one to reach out to and share my grief with. In that moment, God convicted me to start a support group at our church for families who had experienced the loss of a pregnancy or an infant.

I had attended two support meetings elsewhere for pregnancy and infant loss, but I was still very much in the midst of my own grief. The thought of starting a support group when I was so vulnerable made no sense to me, but it became difficult to avoid the calling God had put on my heart. He continued to break my heart for what broke His. While driving to work one day, I was overwhelmed by tears, not for my own loss but the loss of others, knowing that so many people suffered in silence.

I was able to connect with a friend from church who had experienced two miscarriages. We sat in the corner of a coffee shop and exchanged our stories of grief. It was reassuring to know that everything I was feeling—all the anger, guilt, emptiness, and hopelessness—had been experienced by her as well. For the first time since my loss, I felt normal. I was so thankful to have a friend who understood exactly what I was feeling and knew what I was experiencing.

We continued our conversations via email and brainstormed about what a support group for pregnancy loss might look like. We agreed that infant loss and infertility should be included as well.

Again in Pastor Kathy's office, I told her about the weight on my heart for others who had lost their children. She had been in the chain of brainstorming emails about the support group and offered pastoral support for the group. "Do you know of anyone who would be able to lead such a group? Perhaps your counsellor would know someone?" she asked.

"I'm not sure, but I could ask."

"It should probably be someone who has experienced the loss of a child."

"Yes, it would definitely have to be someone who has had the experience and understands the loss."

"Well, we can pray about it."

I took a long pause and a deep breath before muttering, "I can do it."

I had never felt so unequipped for anything. Never had I imagined leading a group for grieving parents. I would much rather be on a stage in front of thousands of people to perform dance choreography or discuss strategies to support child development for classroom and home settings. Facilitating a group for the most devastating experience I've endured in my life—of course that's what God would call me to do! While I felt completely incapable of planning for a group of this capacity, it was that exact reason I accepted God's invitation to do so. I recognized that it was not by my own desires or plans that this idea came to light. It was something that my Heavenly Father trusted me with. I was fearful and humbled as I walked in obedience to His calling.

There was urgency on our hearts for this support group. We were following God's prompting. The support group began the following month, identified as "Unwritten Stories: finding hope in the unwritten chapter of parenting, a Christian support group for those who have experienced miscarriage, stillbirth, infant loss, or infertility." Since there were other support groups and grief counselling available through hospitals and mental health associations, we decided to create a Christian support group where men and women could feel safe to share their frustrations with God as well as their stories of faith.[2]

In a season when I didn't feel like I was talking to God much, He sure was talking to me. As a spirit-led person, my ears and heart were still open to receiving Him. I'm thankful that I was still able to hear clearly—and boy, was His voice loud!

As the months passed, God gave me the courage to tell people about my miscarriage when they asked if I planned to have another child. I didn't have the capacity to lie, and I couldn't hold the grief of losing a child any longer. It was too painful. Sometimes the words came out gracefully; other times I could only blurt out "I recently had a miscarriage" and run in the opposite direction.

Brian and I gained the confidence to talk more openly about our experience, and to our surprise, people opened up to us about their losses. People who had been my friends for years would tell me about their miscarriages and how they would always carry their losses with them. The world would forget and move on, but as parents, we would always carry our lost child's memory with us.

My conversations with God continued, and I slowly found a heart of worship again. It was at this point in our journey, three months after losing Malakai, when God put it on our hearts to try to conceive again.

---

2 A complete list of resources is available on page 87.

chapter twelve

The Road to Conception

WHEN WE DECIDED TO EXPAND OUR FAMILY BEYOND HUSBAND and wife, we weren't worried about conception. We expected that it would take at least a few months, but with Maliya and Malakai, we were able to conceive within the first month of trying. This time, my body was giving me signs of ovulation long before we were emotionally ready to conceive again.

I got mad at myself. "Thank you, body, for reminding me that I'm no longer pregnant and that you are ready to procreate while my heart is so far from being in that place."

At first Brian was afraid of getting too close for fear of hurting me. When we finally reached the emotional place of being ready, we were terrified. What if the miscarriage had caused damage? What if we couldn't conceive? What if it would take a really long time because my body was different now?

We didn't conceive the first month we tried, and I couldn't help but cry. I was used to seeing that positive sign after only one month, but it didn't happen this time. So much hope was put into getting pregnant again, and I felt like we failed and that hope was pulled out from beneath me again. All the fears I had about not being able to conceive came rushing to the surface.

Around us were signs of celebration. Christmas was drawing near, which meant more social gatherings, family dinners, and happiness everywhere. We were just trying to survive. By this time, our friends and families knew what we were going through. Even though we had the support of everyone around us, I still felt guilty for not being able to join in the celebrations of our Saviour's birth. People would wish me "Merry Christmas" and I'd reply, "Thank you; good morning."

In November, I had begun having panic attacks. By Christmas, my panic attacks were frequent and heightened, lasting for twenty or thirty minutes. My heart raced, my temperature rose, my breath caught, my stomach wrenched, my skin tingled, and I felt like I was going to pass out. The panic attacks would come out of nowhere, often did not have a trigger, and would exhaust me for the remainder of the day. Recovering meant going home and sleeping off the spike my nervous system had just endured.

Christmas was another reminder of our loss. I would've been twenty-four weeks pregnant and able to announce whether we were expecting a boy or a girl. Instead, reminders were everywhere that my womb was empty. I'm so thankful for my family, who kept Maliya occupied during our family's Christmas dinner. Brian and I hid in a different room and watched a movie, which was a great escape from the reality that we were facing. When we came home from Christmas dinner I asked Brian to please take down the Christmas tree. It was definitely a record, having the tree and all the decorations put away by 10:30 Christmas night.

Maliya's birthday was happening in a week's time, and that gave us something to look forward to. At the same time, I was anxious, thinking about being in a room full of people and having to make small talk. The party was small, and everyone there knew about our situation, but depression and anxiety made it hard for me to connect with family and friends despite my greatest efforts. In hindsight, it was no wonder we weren't able to conceive the second month either. We were highly stressed and still very much in the midst of our grief.

Watching Brian grieve was difficult. He isolated himself and pulled away from me to try to protect me from what he was feeling. I had never seen him so angry with God. He stopped praying with Maliya and me and stopped attending church on Sundays. Friends would reach out, but he declined invitations. He was more wounded than I was, and it was challenging to support him while I was so low myself. I wanted to "fix" him, but at the same time, I knew it wasn't my place. All I could do was pray and have faith that God would meet Brian where he was and gently bring him out of the darkness.

He wanted his wife back, and I wondered where my husband had gone. Grief really does change people, and we were learning how to find ourselves and how to find each other. We were walking parallel paths on the same journey, looking over at one another, knowing the pain without knowing the experience.

Our paths met after a long three months of walking alone. Baby-making became more relaxed and felt less like a chore. We accepted this new road we were on and took the pressure off ourselves to conceive. We would do our part and leave the rest up to God.

Here are two of my journal entries from our third month of trying:

March 14, 2015

This afternoon I realized that it's been one year since the car accident. In 365 days a lot has happened! We've been trying to conceive since December, and I was trying not to get discouraged. My sense of taste has been off for the past two weeks, starting at day 20, when I thought I could be pregnant. Tested at day 24 and it came back negative. Tested again at day 27, negative. I was so frustrated since I've been overly tired as well.

Today is day 32, was going to test again in the morning, but I couldn't wait—it's positive! I knew my body wouldn't lie, but unlike the first two, there's been no nausea or heightened sense of smell, yet. I'm four weeks and three days today. Praying we get to hold this one.

Brian and I were thrilled to be expecting again, but knowing too well that the pregnancy could suddenly end without warning robbed us of the happiness we had had the first two times we found out we were expecting. We stood in the bathroom, holding each other, staring at the positive test without speaking, knowing exactly how each other felt.

March 20, 2015

When Maliya woke up this morning, the first thing she said was, "How come there's a baby in your tummy?" I asked her who told her that. She said, "Mommy." I said, "No, I didn't." Then she said, "Daddy," with uncertainty in her voice. No one told her. Did God tell her in her dreams? She just woke and asked.

Had my first prenatal check up with Dr. J yesterday. I was her last patient of the day, so all the doors in the office were left open. I heard her review my pregnancy test from the other room, and she let out, "Yay!" Then she walked into the room, saw me, and said "Yay" again while clapping her hands together with happiness for us. She said she was happy to see my name on her patient list today as a prenatal appointment. Ultrasound is on April 17. Praying for a heartbeat.

Had a session with Juliana today and shared my fears for this pregnancy. We spent a large part of the time talking about faith versus fear. I said they couldn't exist together, and she challenged me on that. My homework is to invite God into the fear, rather than just pulling myself out and rebuking the fear. Juliana said my fear is genuine. I agreed.

We told friends shortly after we knew that we were expecting again. Our Bible study group knew, my mentors knew, and we asked for as much prayer coverage as we could get. My anxiety was high, and my faith was low. Sometimes my prayers were only a few sentences, and that's all I could bring to God. The miscarriage had made me enter a more authentic relationship with God. Before, I didn't feel right being angry with Him or letting Him know how I really felt (as if I could hide the truth from Him). Now I allowed myself to experience my feelings, resulting in a growing, deepening relationship with my Creator and discovering where His will met mine.

chapter thirteen

Pink

AT ONE DAY SHY OF SEVEN WEEKS PREGNANT, I HAD THE LARGE task of hosting a fundraiser at work. We were expecting about fifty people to attend our art auction and silent auction to help raise funds toward a new playground structure.

I went to the bathroom before the event and was horrified when I saw a streak of pink. "No, Lord," I pleaded. "No, no, no. Please don't let this happen again!"

Immediately I sent a text message to Brian and asked him to pray. He and Maliya arrived about thirty minutes later, which helped me stay calm and somehow focus on the fundraising event. I pulled myself out of every emotion I had, allowing my mind to overpower my heart. There was no time to be panicked, anxious, worried, terrified, or sad with so many of my preschool families present.

Three hours later, I arrived at home, hoping that the pink had stopped. It hadn't. In fact, things got worse, and I had mild cramps that evening. There were no words to describe what I was feeling. Could everything possibly be happening all over again?

As I lay in bed that night, Brian prayed over me. Then we were silent as tears streamed down my face. My body was telling me something my heart didn't want to accept and my mind wanted to deny. The stream of tears grew into a body-convulsing downpour, snot started to drip uncontrollably out of my nose, and I was beyond all chance of composure. Brian got up to get a tissue for me, but all I could do was tuck it between my face and my pillow and leave it there. There was no possibility of wiping away my tears or the fear that resonated to my core. I fell asleep out of pure exhaustion, the tissue clinging to my face and my heart clinging to what little hope I had left.

I woke the next morning with Maliya next to me (like every morning, since she finds her way into our bed each night). Brian had already left for work, and I lay there staring at my daughter, watching her sleep and thinking, *What if she's my only one? What if God means for us to only have one child on earth?*

My phone buzzed with a text message from Brian. He asked how I was doing and tried to reassure me that the cramps could be my uterus stretching to accommodate the growing baby. Having been pregnant before, I knew what stretching felt like and wished what I was feeling was just an uncomfortable stretch.

My parents came over to babysit Maliya that morning. Mom took one look at me and asked if I was all right. I told her I had started spotting the previous night. She was at a loss for words but walked around saying, "It's going to be okay; everything is going to be okay." I wasn't sure if she was telling me or herself, as I was avoiding eye contact.

I was afraid to go to the bathroom. When I did, I saw that the pink had changed to red. "Noooo," I cried out to God. "No, no, no, please no, God!" My fingers stumbled as I sent a text message to Brian. "I'm bleeding."

I dragged myself to my room, sat on the edge of the bed, and cried. There was no denying what was happening. Again.

My vision was blurred from the tears, and in that moment Maliya came to find me. She crawled up in my lap and rested. Holding her toward my chest, I clutched her tightly and cried into her. As I tenderly held my firstborn in my arms, I was saying good-bye to my third.

Maliya was wrapped around me. I shook from crying so hard, yet I could hear her giggling from the quaking of my body. When I pulled her away from me, our eyes met. She saw my tears and immediately frowned.

"How come you're crying?"

"Mommy is really sad."

Maliya began to whine and cry with me. I asked my mom to please take Maliya from me, but she wouldn't leave my side. My mom tried to comfort me, but it was useless. The more I tried to hand Maliya to my mom, the more my daughter fought, and now Maliya was in full-blown tears.

Maliya reached for me and climbed back into my arms, and all I could do was hold her and cry. No words were necessary. She knew my heart was heavy, and in her loving three-year-old way, she was there to cry with me.

Time seemed to be standing still and simultaneously robbing me of moments with my baby. Eventually I made it back downstairs. Brian was home soon after to take me to the hospital.

chapter fourteen

The Emergency Room

RELUCTANTLY I SLITHERED OUT OF THE CAR AND DRAGGED myself toward the big red letters that read "EMERGENCY."

"Care card and ID please. What are you here for?"

"I think I'm miscarrying."

"Bleeding?"

"Spotting and cramping."

"Since when?"

"Last night, and it got heavier this morning."

"Who is your family doctor?"

"Dr. J."

"Right wrist please," and with that I was admitted. I found a seat on the far right side of the room and sank into the worn blue chairs, noticing the dark stains on them.

Shortly after I sat down, an elderly man wearing a mask and holding a vomit bucket sat beside me. In a room full of empty chairs, he chose to sit right next to me. I'm sure he wasn't feeling up to walking any farther in his condition, but I'm slightly germophobic (or extremely germophobic, if you ask my husband). Working with children has made me conscious of germs. Now, don't get me wrong; I absolutely love working with young children. Self-care and hygiene are skills we discuss daily with them. However, there have been times when I've excused myself from the classroom to wash my eyes out after being sneezed on. Wiping noses and bums and cleaning up vomit are skills I should really add to my resume, along with the fact that I'm an impeccable hand-washer. You can imagine how my insides jittered when Mr. Vomit Bucket sat next to me. I timidly excused myself and retreated to the far left side of the room.

Brian found his way to me after parking the car a few blocks away. Even in an emergency, we refused to pay the hospital parking rates. The triage nurses were calling out names, and patients seemed to be disappearing. The nurses were joking that they should start calling the names like they were lottery winners.

When my name was called, the nurse looked at Brian and asked, "Is this your... boyfriend?" I always joked with Brian that people would think we're teenage parents, and this proved it.

"Is this your first pregnancy?"

"My third."

"Do you have any children?"

"Yes, a daughter."

The nurse tried to calm me down by telling me that a friend of hers had a healthy baby after bleeding for six months of her pregnancy. "You're not happy," she said. I shook my head. "Of course not. I know this is a hard time, but let's get you checked out and see what's going on."

Bed 32: the fluorescent lights above, dirty spotted white tiles beneath, ticking of a clock, and buzzing of machines from other rooms surrounded me as I slipped into an oversized blue hospital gown. I looked around the room and noticed drawers that were labelled "Sanitary Pads," "Forceps," "Speculums," and "Gloves." My present reality tormented my heart. Like the used needles I saw across from me, being at the hospital penetrated me with pain, injecting uncertainty and fear.

I heard screeching wheels coming down the hallway, making their way to my room. The phlebotomist and her assistant had arrived to take my blood. The assistant threw five vials into the collection tray and then leaned against the wall and put her hands in her pockets. I wanted to be there just as much as she apparently did.

"Which arm would you like?"

"Left, please."

"Make a fist. Are you ready? Okay, one, two, three." The phlebotomist poked me, but no blood came out, which was a first for me. She jiggled the needle around like a key jammed inside of a lock. When that didn't work, she tilted the needle up and down, left and right, and then started using it like a joystick while it was still penetrating my arm. "Oh, it's just that they need five samples."

That's fine, I thought, *I'm willing to give it to you, but please stop cruising through my arm like a winding road map.*

She then went to the other arm. "Wow, look at that vein! I should've checked this side in the first place." I wasn't sure if that comment was supposed to reassure me.

My blood samples were taken, and the phlebotomist said, "Okay, just let me check your hospital bracelet." She then double-checked my name and birthdate. Good thing she took my blood *before* she checked! Thankfully the requisition was right and I was the victim she was looking for.

Next came a doctor with a portable ultrasound machine. He was extremely gentle and compassionate. "We'll have to send you for a more detailed ultrasound; I can't see much on this machine beyond bowel gas." Non-performing veins, gassy bowels—my body was working against me through the miscarriage and was still refusing to co-operate for the examinations.

Two hours later, I arrived in the ultrasound room. But my bladder wasn't full enough and obstructed the view of my uterus. *Come on, body, can't you just do one thing right?* I could wait until their next available appointment, hours away, or have an internal ultrasound performed. Waiting was not an option for my sanity. I went with the invasive option.

As I lay there in the ultrasound room, my heart grew dim and matched the darkness of the room. To my left was a poster with week-by-week fetal development, something I knew I wouldn't get to experience in the coming months. My heart grew darker and darker. Holding in the tears to make it through the ultrasound, I looked up through the white ceiling and asked God to take this from me.

Brian was standing next to me when the ultrasound technician said, "There's still a yolk sac in there, but it's measuring smaller than seven weeks, so there's no heartbeat. It could mean that it's just early, and, if you ovulated later, it may be too early to detect a heartbeat." Again a piece of hope was being offered to me, but I was slowly losing grip on it. Since we were actively trying to conceive, I knew my dates were correct and that I hadn't ovulated late.

Two more hours passed, and still no doctor had come with the results. But I had all the information I needed. I asked the nurse who had checked me in four hours earlier if I could please go home. She told me to wait and that the doctor would be coming soon. She apologized as well. "Sorry, we had someone pass out." I understood how a person who lost consciousness would take priority. I was breathing—at least I think I was; my heart was beating; I was somewhat coherent; but what about the life that was growing inside of me? Wasn't my baby's life worth saving? Could someone please revive the life within me?

Earlier in the morning we had heard a code yellow being called over the intercom, which meant a patient had gone missing. I was contemplating pulling a code yellow. My patience was running low, I was hungry, and my heart was reaching its capacity for being able to survive.

A new nurse came in and told me that the doctor would have to do a pelvic exam. She then looked at me and asked, "Is the pelvic exam for you?" This made me question if she was actually a nurse, as I doubted the doctor would be trying to examine my husband's cervix, but somehow I calmly replied, "Yes, the pelvic exam is for me."

By the time the nurse had prepared me for the pelvic exam, I was completely drained. My heart began to overpower my mind, and I could no longer deny what was happening. I lay there on the exam table waiting for the doctor, scrunched in a ball on my side while tears flooded down my face. Reality entered, and hope exited.

Brian grabbed what he could find to soak up my tears just as the doctor and nurse entered to begin my exam. "I'm just going to check if your cervix is open to see—" The doctor didn't have to finish his sentence; I knew he wanted to see if I was going into labour. No ounce of dignity was left in me.

The nurse kept asking if I was okay, apologizing for the discomfort, and telling me the exam would be over soon. Unless they could heal a broken heart, nothing was okay. Even after the exam was completed, all I could do was lie there and cry.

Somehow I managed to get dressed and waited for the doctor to discharge me. He returned and reported that the ultrasound showed that the gestational sac only measured around five weeks and that my HCG (human chorionic gonadotropin) levels were quite low for being seven weeks' pregnant. "The ultrasound isn't enough information, but with the bloodwork, there's a 90 percent chance that you're having a miscarriage. I can't say 100 percent, because it's so early. You'll probably start to cramp more and have heavier bleeding in the next few days."

I lived in the 90 percent. Having 10 percent of hope would be too painful. The doctor discharged me with a requisition for a follow-up ultrasound the next week.

chapter fifteen

Keone

OVER THE NEXT TWENTY-FOUR HOURS I SOMEHOW FOUND THE strength to text and email many in our support system for prayer coverage: my mentors, my close friends, our Bible study group, and our pastors. We didn't have the capacity to keep the loss to ourselves this time. God surrounded us with community, and the response was overwhelming. It was the only reason I knew we had not been forsaken. My phone didn't stop buzzing with text messages, emails were constant, and cards came to our door along with meals and flowers.

I felt physically weak, emotionally broken, and spiritually scattered. Nothing made sense, and time froze, though as each day passed, my cramps increased, and I finally realized they were no longer cramps. They were contractions. After twenty-four hours of contractions I knew that the 10 percent of hope no longer existed. We lost our third child over Easter weekend.

Brian took Maliya out for most of the weekend, allowing me to rest. The carnival was in town, and though Maliya was still too small to go on any of the rides, she came home with an armful of carnival prizes and goodies from the toy store. I joked that Brian didn't even take me on elaborate dates like that. He said, "I have to tell you something Maliya said while we were out," but before he could tell me, Maliya pulled me in the opposite direction. When she finally settled in with her new toys, I asked Brian to tell me about his conversation with her.

"While we were shopping, we went through the baby section, and Maliya said she wanted to buy something for the baby." My tears began to fall at this point. "I told her that the baby had to go to heaven, and she replied, 'Not that one. The one in Mommy's tummy.'" I couldn't see through my tears anymore, and I just sat on the couch until I was completely empty. How were we going to tell our three-year-old that we had lost another baby?

Depleted from the events of the weekend, Brian and I stood in our kitchen that Monday night trying to make sense of life. I turned to him and asked, "How are we going to do this again? How are we going to name another baby we won't get to hold?"

This little life that had touched us for only seven weeks left me thinking about rays of light. Brian said he had been seeing visions of stars. It seemed to me that God was putting pieces of heaven on our hearts. He was letting us know that our little one was with Him.

We stood there, leaning over our kitchen counter, looking through names that meant light, heaven, and stars. Nothing really resonated, and I was close to suggesting that we wait. We didn't want to force the choice, and when a name affected our hearts, we would know. Just then Brian read out, "Keone. It's a unisex Hawaiian name that means 'the homeland.'"

I couldn't speak. My heart leapt out of my chest, and I collapsed into Brian's arms and cried uncontrollably. As he held me, Brian whispered, "I think that really spoke to you."

"Keone. Keone, our light guiding us back to the homeland."

chapter sixteen

The Aftermath

I DRAGGED MY BODY AROUND FOR MORE THAN A WEEK. I FELT like an infant, only being able to do an hour of activity before having to crawl back into bed and sleep. No matter how much sleep I got, I didn't feel rested, and I remained dizzy and disoriented.

I decided to check myself into the emergency room again, thinking that I had lost too much blood and that could be the reason for the dizziness. Even though I had an appointment with Dr. J the following day, I couldn't wait any longer for answers. I accepted my mom's offer to drive me to the hospital for a follow-up ultrasound.

My mom stayed in the waiting room until Brian arrived. Alone in the hospital room, I received the news that my uterus was all clear. While that was an answered prayer (I didn't want to do a round of misoprostol or require a D and C), the news left me crippled in the chair.

My baby was gone. Every last bit of the life I carried had departed the earth, and I was left behind. The room spun around me, and I was trapped in the middle, whirling in my tears, spiralling into a pit of anguish. Losing two children in seven months is beyond a human's capacity to handle. God had officially given me more than I could bear. Tears fell until my head pounded.

Thankfully, in that moment Brian found me. One week before we'd been able to joke at the hospital; now the only thing we could do was stare hopelessly at each other in silence while we waited for my blood test results.

My red blood cell and hemoglobin counts were indeed low, but not low enough to require a transfusion. As the doctor gave me my results, the sound of her voice was muted by my devastation. "Miscarriage. Trauma. Body. Time. Recover." I left, depleted and hopeless.

Dr. J followed up with me the next afternoon to review my ultrasound and blood work. Walking into the room with a furrowed brow and a sigh of sadness for me, she let out an "Oh, Steffie." I tried to describe the symptoms of my body, which had never felt this way before, and commented that something must be wrong. "Your hemoglobin is at 112, but that number wouldn't be giving you the fatigue you're describing. It's the depression."

Those words were a definite blow while I was already down. My depression had never been debilitating, not until this point.

She asked if I needed any notes for work, had any questions, or needed anything else. I shook my head. "You know where to find me. Just call if you need anything." Physically, nothing was worrisome; however, my mental and emotional states were holding my body captive, dragging me behind.

I don't know how I found the courage to email my supervisor at work to let him know the truth behind me taking "sick" time. Preschool registration for the following school year was less than a week away, but he told me to take care of myself and not to worry about anything at work.

In the fall, I had attended a women's retreat, and in a break-out group I talked about my first loss. One of the women suggested that I tell one person at work, just one. That way, if I was having a rough day or something triggered my grief, I could send a silent signal to excuse myself. She spoke from the experience of losing a child herself. I hadn't had the strength to do that the first time, and there were days when I really could have used a silent rescue. This time, I couldn't hold the loss to myself, and I asked my supervisor to share the news with the rest of the supervisory team. I needed lifesavers from all angles. I didn't know if one person could save me if I were drowning; I needed a team, standing on the sidelines ready to reach out to me.

A few co-workers emailed me with their condolences, and I was very grateful for support from the office staff. Though I continued to take time off, a weight had been lifted, knowing that a piece of my truth had been shared with my colleagues. I knew that when I returned to work, they'd understand the limits of my functionality.

Anxiety rose as my counselling session that week drew near. To this point, I had broken the news of our second loss through writing, in emails and text messages. Counselling would mean that I would have to say it out loud.

My hands were sweating as I drove to my appointment, and my heart began beating faster the closer I got to my destination. As I climbed the stairs to Juliana's office, the fear of having to talk out loud about our loss choked me.

I handed Juliana the two poems I had written that week and said, "I'm so nervous to be here. I've had a rough go."

Her eyes grew wide with concern as she replied, "Do you need gentleness today?"

"Yes, please."

I sat in the cushioned chair and felt it surrounding me, but no part of me was present. I opened my mouth to speak, but no words came out; instead I was gasping for air. My right arm rested on my knee, holding the weight of my head, which was resting in my hand as I tried to prevent myself from collapsing.

Minutes passed, and I couldn't speak. I couldn't even make eye contact. Finally I blurted out, "I miscarried again."

Silence.

Juliana spoke in a tone and volume that was barely audible. "I was afraid you were going to say that. I'm so sorry." She gave me permission to disconnect from my emotions as much as I needed to that session in order to unpack my story, and she asked how it was even possible for me to sit there and share. I honestly had no idea.

We learn from experience. Unfortunately for me, I had gone through this once before. Sadly, I knew roughly how to navigate through the trauma. Taking time off work and making time for myself were priorities for me this time, something I didn't allow myself to have the first time.

The whole session was a blur. I was on the verge of tears for the entire hour. Water rose to my eyes but never fell. Juliana would usually have me read one of my poems to take me to that emotional place and try to connect, but that day she looked at my words on the pages and said, "Just by glancing at these, I can see how potent they are. We'll come back to these another day." She wiped the tears that fell from her eyes and told me to be gentle with myself that week. I knew she had to have been thinking of her two young children during our time together. A mother's heart is where her children are. Pieces of my heart were torn between heaven and earth.

chapter seventeen

Happy Birthday

"WHAT'S MALAKAI DOING IN HEAVEN?" MALIYA ASKED ME ONE night as we were lying in her bed.

"What do you think he's doing?"

"Is he playing?"

"I don't know; what do you think?"

"Is Malakai sleeping in heaven? Does he have a crib? Does he poo-poo in his diaper?"

I lay there in silence, listening to her pondering heaven. It was too painful to think of answers and maintain the conversation. As much as I wanted to be curious with her, it hurt too much, knowing that he'd never sleep in my arms and there would be no diapers to change.

Maliya then asked something that nearly left me needing chest compressions. "Where's his mommy and daddy?"

My sorrow leapt from my heart into my throat, but I forced it back down in order to answer my daughter. "He has the same mommy and daddy as you. We're here." Acknowledging the separation and having to say it out loud felt like daggers piercing my heart. My throat tightened, and sorrow leaked from my eyes, one drop at a time.

"Are you his mommy? Is his daddy Brian? Does he want to come here?"

"Yes, we're his mommy and daddy, just like we're your mommy and daddy. You're his big sister. We can only go there; he won't be coming here. We can go to heaven only when Jesus tells us it's our time to go."

This conversation, like others with her, tore me in half. But I was thankful for the opportunity to help Maliya process who Malakai was, and it helped me process our loss as well. At the same time, I was often blindsided by her questions. She usually asked at random times without warning, whipping my heart into the midst of grief. I often saw myself with both of my arms outstretched, one reaching down, holding Maliya here on earth, and the other reaching to heaven, longing to hold the hands of Malakai and Keone.

There was no time for me to catch my breath or digest our conversation before Maliya's next question. "How come you were sad, Mommy?"

I breathed in courage, and my words trembled as they left my lips. "You know the baby that was in Mommy's tummy? It had to go to heaven too."

"How come you were crying?"

"Because I didn't want the baby to go; I wanted it to stay longer."

"Is it gonna cry?"

"No, there are no tears in heaven. It's a happy place."

"I want to go there."

"Me too. We will one day. Would you like to know the baby's name?"

Maliya nodded and waited patiently for me. I found the strength to say, "Keone."

"Keone?"

"Yup, Keone. The baby is with Malakai in heaven."

"Is it a she?"

"I don't know; we didn't get to find out. Do you think Keone is a she?"

"Yeah."

"I think so too," I whispered.

Waking the next morning, I willed myself to begin the day—April 15, my original due date. Repeatedly I told myself that I would make it through the day, but I didn't even make it to breakfast. When my parents arrived, I allowed myself to hand over my parenting responsibilities and found myself walking aimlessly around the kitchen.

I was foolish to think I could will myself into any type of normalcy. A baby should have been in my arms. My arms were empty, my womb was empty, and I lacked the ability to function. Retreating upstairs, I put on my headphones, drowned out the world with songs that brought me closer to my two angels, and cried until I had nothing left.

Depleted of sadness, anger, grief, and agony, I disconnected myself from my heart and returned to the kitchen. My body was making toast, but my mind was completely numb. Sitting at the dining table, I stared down at two pieces of brown bread covered in peanut butter and strawberry jam. I had no desire to eat, no desire to drink, and was thankful that breathing and blood flow were involuntary. My parents' voices buzzed around my head. Maliya's laughter zipped through my ears, yet I was nowhere to be found. Only my body was present.

I needed air. I needed an escape. I kissed Maliya goodbye, cut a few white flowers from our garden, got in the car, and drove toward the water. I feel as though the sea understands me, and it's where my internal emotional raging meets the calm surface I'm used to portraying. White flowers had been a part of my mourning journey, representing purity and grace. Taking pictures of white flowers was one way I spent time with my two babies I couldn't hold.

I climbed over washed-up logs and found my way down to the beach. The damp sand stuck to the bottom of my runners, leaving an imprint of the path I had travelled. Gently I placed my two white flowers on a log and captured an image of the way the petals danced as they were grazed by the wind and the shadows beneath them that were cast by the sun, which shone brightly that day.

One week after losing Malakai. I would've been eleven weeks pregnant, marked by the lines on the bench.

Scattered petals represented the trail of my grief.

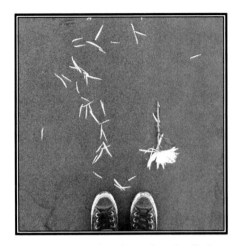

Somehow I still remained standing in the midst of brokenness.

Reaching out to heaven.

During a quiet walk and time of reflection.

A foggy winter morning before heading to work.

The fence was a reminder that there will always be a division between heaven and earth, between my babies and I.

The wooden boat we purchased in memory of Malakai.

*Mother's Day. Maliya's hand, holding symbols of our angels
who never got to bloom here on earth.*

It was Malakai's birth day. Though I missed Keone greatly, most of my time was spent wondering about Malakai, what he would have looked like, what his voice would have sounded like, the way his eyes would have squinted when they met mine for the first time. I walked the beach, having conversations with heaven that stirred up my heart and settled my spirit. Somehow I survived the day.

That evening I wrote this in my journal:

I thought I could do it. I thought I could make it through the day. Mom brought flowers for the table, "To cheer you up today, and for some colour." I thanked her and said I wanted my white flowers. I couldn't handle today, I was supposed to be holding a baby, instead I hold memories of two who couldn't be here. Went to take pictures with white flowers and Malakai's boat. That made a world of a difference, could finally function and start my day. Maliya wanted to get Malakai a cupcake. We stopped into a bakery and settled on a brownie. "I can share the nuts with Malakai. Is he gonna come?" I told her we could only go there, he couldn't come back. "When Jesus comes to get us, then we can go to heaven. I want to go there." B and I agreed we want to go too, where our family of five can be together. Happy birthday, Malakai. We love you, and we'll be there soon.

I'm in agony each day I'm without Malakai and Keone, and I feel that God is telling me the same thing. It pains Him to be physically separated from us, watching us from heaven, no longer able to be together on earth. He wants to meet us in our suffering.

Our stories are to be heard, and our pain deserves a voice. God wants to sit with us in the midst of our pain. He wants to meet us in the pit of our anguish. Whether we feel like we need to blame Him for our suffering or have His arms surround us in comfort, His presence is with us. In our broken world, we will continue to face trials, and Jesus reminds us that "In this world you will have trouble. But take heart! I have overcome the world" (John 16:33).

chapter eighteen

Hope, Love and Light

Know that your true nature is love. Love in its many forms binds the universe together. All pain exists to bring our attention to the places in our lives that need more love and gratitude. Be grateful for your ability to feel pain. It allows you to bring the love that you are into the darkest places in your life. Know that as you breathe in more and more love, you will be able to release more and more pain.[3]

IT'S BEEN TWO WEEKS SINCE THE SECOND MISCARRIAGE. OUR recent experiences have taught us to hold things of this world more loosely, even our children, which feels like an impossible task.

God showed me a vision of myself before we lost Keone. I was kneeling at the feet of Jesus, holding a baby in my arms, sobbing. Jesus was asking me to hand my baby over to Him. Though

---

3 Christiane Northrup, "You Have to Feel It to Heal It," *Shambhala Sun* (September 2004), 19.

this image had already been forced in the natural world, my spirit was holding on to what was taken from me.

I couldn't comprehend just how much Jesus was really asking of me. I now see myself at His feet with my two babies, one in each arm, head hanging in despair. Jesus is waiting patiently for me, knowing how hard it is for me to pass my babies over to rest with Him. I don't feel rushed; I don't feel bullied; I feel Jesus meeting me right where I am, in the midst of missing my children. He grieves with me and stands over me to protect me while I'm in this season of loss and vulnerability.

I'm clutching my children tightly, holding them close to me, but God is asking me to set them free, because when my arms are full of the things I want, He can't place in my care the things *He* wants.

Heaven is so much closer than it used to be. Pieces of me are scattered between two realms. Though I wish I knew the reasons why all my children can't be here with me, I know that no answer in this world will satisfy me. I was created to chase after heaven. Each day I will put on my armour, set foot on the battlefield, and make a conscious decision to chase hope, love, and light. Will you join me?

Epilogue

While pregnant with Keone, I had a dream. I remember nothing except for a girl's name. The name was nearly audible and woke me from my sleep. It was at that moment that I knew God was promising us a baby girl. I thought Keone was that promise, but God's plan was greater still.

Two months after the loss of Keone, I was pregnant again and terrified. I didn't know if I would survive another loss, and finding the strength to think positively proved to be challenging. Due to the consecutive pregnancy losses, I was sent for ultrasounds every two weeks during the first trimester. It was a high-risk pregnancy that included hemorrhaging of the gestational sac and marginal placenta previa. My depression also reached its peak as a side effect to the anti-nausea medication I was prescribed.

It was difficult to be excited about the pregnancy when I felt that my body had failed me twice before. I had trouble connecting with the baby, even when I felt movement within my womb. One distinct memory I have was Brian wanting to set up the nursery. I told him not to, admitting that I couldn't bear to see everything be set up only to come down if we lost this baby too. Anxiety paralyzed me. I lived from one doctor's appointment to the next, having momentary assurance of the life within me when I heard the baby's heartbeat.

Maliya's faith in the pregnancy kept me believing that I'd carry the baby to term and have a safe labour and delivery. She'd often approach me to hug my belly or have conversations with the baby. Maliya frequently sat with her hands on my belly, giggled when the baby kicked, and told the baby, "Don't worry, I'm here."

The name I heard in my dream was *Kailani*. Ten months after the loss of Keone, we welcomed a healthy baby girl into our lives. Her name is Kailani. *Kai* means sea, representing the rough waters we have travelled. *Lani* means sky or heaven. She is our promised gift from above, completing our family in heaven and on earth.

Kailani is now one month old and growing quickly. Maliya is so in love with her baby sister and has plans for all the things they're going to do when they "grow bigger, like teenagers." It has been amazing to witness the instant bond between my daughters.

Having two children on earth makes me feel less torn between two realms. Our family is now complete with two girls and two angels. My grief has changed but has not ended. I believe my grief will continue to evolve for as long as I live. The flowers blooming in the spring remind me of Malakai. The stars on a clear winter's night remind me of Keone.

Maliya often talks about the babies in heaven. Just today she drew a picture of me and said, "That's you when you had Malakai in your tummy." The unexpected conversations about my angels no longer sting my heart as deeply, and I cherish each moment I get to talk about them.

I have always wanted four children; it just looks different than I imagined. We are a family of six. There are four of us on earth continually chasing the light of heaven until the day we can all walk together on the other side of eternity.

> *Let us hold tightly without wavering to the hope we affirm, for God can be trusted to keep his promise.*

—Hebrews 10:23 NLT

Acknowledgements

This book was a download from heaven and wrote itself as life unfolded. I would've never been able to complete this memoir if it were not for many supportive people in my life.

Brian—Thank you for not even hesitating when I brought up the idea of writing a book and sharing our story. Your support and encouragement is what keeps me going each day. Thanks for keeping Maliya occupied for countless hours so I could get all these words on a page. I love you more than I thought was possible. Thanks for sailing through each storm with me. You're my everything.

Maliya—Your understanding of what our family has been through is beyond your years. The revelations of heaven you continue to share amaze me. Thank you for remembering to talk about the babies and for making me laugh. It's a privilege to be your mommy. I love you always.

My parents—Thank you for being supportive of my writing and encouraging me to write this story. Mom and Uncle Dave, thanks for dedicating your retirement to caring for Maliya (and now Kailani). Your support through each pregnancy has been invaluable.

Jeremy—You are my eyes into the Kingdom. Thanks for the long emails and the encouraging Scripture and for being my prayer warrior. I'm so grateful for your shoulder to lean on and for your words of wisdom.

Marites, Jessica, and Michelle—You three have been my lifeline. Thank you for the long chats, emails, and text messages that kept me going. Your prayers mean more than you know. I'm thankful the Lord has blessed me with your friendships.

Janice, Mrs. Sundell, Brenda, and David—Thank you for helping me get my manuscript ready for the writing competition that made this book possible.

Mark and Marnie—Thank you for consulting on the manuscript and pointing me in the right direction.

ECE Mom Community—I enjoy connecting with each one of you and appreciate all the conversations we have. Thank you for journeying with my family and for reading our stories.

Resources

Unwritten Stories Support Group

A Christian support group for those who have
experienced miscarriage, stillbirth, infant loss or infertility,
finding hope in the unwritten chapter of parenting.

The Tapestry Church:
www.thetapestry.ca/care

Empty Cradle Support Group

Support for parents who have experienced the
loss of an infant or failed pregnancy.

www.emptycradle.bc.ca

Juliana Fruhling, MA-MAFT, Registered Clinical Counsellor

Cedar Springs Counselling, Vancouver, BC, Canada
www.cedarspringscounselling.com
juliana@cedarspringscounselling.com

Compassionate Friends of Canada

Support for a family when a child dies.

www.tcfcanada.net
1-866-823-0141.

British Columbia Bereavement Helpline

Helping the people of BC cope with grief.

www.bcbereavementhelpline.com
604-738-9950 / 1-877-779-2223

BC Women's Hospital

Recurrent Pregnancy Loss Clinic

www.bcwomens.ca/our-services/gynecology/
recurrent-pregnancy-loss
604-875-3628

Pacific Post Partum Support Society

Providing telephone support, weekly women's support groups, partner education sessions, community trainings and resource materials.

www.postpartum.org

1-855-255-9999

Miscarriage Association

www.miscarriageassociation.org.uk

1-924-200-799

Miscarriage Matters Inc.

www.mymiscarriagematters.com

1-888-520-7743

Still Standing Magazine

www.stillstandingmag.com

PALS - Pregnancy After Loss Support

Choosing hope over fear while nurturing grief.

www.pregnancyafterlosssupport.com

October 15

Pregnancy and Infant Loss Awareness Day.
Resources, articles and events.

www.october15.ca

Pregnancy and Infant Loss Network

www.pailnetwork.ca

About the Author

Stefanie Tong is an early childhood educator, freelance writer, and speaker. As a professional hip hop dancer she has performed at the Vancouver 2010 Winter Olympics closing ceremony and CFL and NFL half time shows and represented Canada at the International Youth Dance Festival in Macau, China. She has earned choreography awards for her work with elementary through university teams, modelling agencies, and numerous dance studios.

After enduring injuries from car accidents that forced her to give up her dance career, Stefanie returned to school and pursued a career in early childhood education. Since 2005 she has been working with non-profit associations, and she is currently the pre-school coordinator for an early years program at a local community centre.

Stefanie's writing journey began after feeling inspired to share the story of her miscarriages. Her writing earned her a spot as a finalist in the 2015 Word Alive Press and Women's Journey of Faith non-fiction manuscript contest. She is now a member of the editorial committee for *The Journal of Early Childhood Educators of British Columbia*.

Stefanie resides with her family in Vancouver, BC, Canada, and enjoys connecting online with her readers, where she shares honestly about grief, pregnancy loss, and parenting.

Connect with Stefanie:

Website: www.stefanie.ca
Blog: www.ecemom.com
Facebook: www.facebook.com/ecemomblog
Instagram: @hi_ecemom
Twitter: @hi_ecemom